Raccoon

Materials:

- gray or white construction paper
  basic mitt puppet—9'' x 12''
    (22.8 x 30.5cm)
    ears—(Cut 2) 3'' x 3'' (7.5 x 7.5cm)
- black construction paper
  mask—4'' x 6'' (10 x 15cm)
  nose—2'' x 2'' (5 x 5cm)
- white construction paper
  eyes—1½'' x 3'' (4 x 7.5cm)

Steps to follow:

Make the basic mitt puppet.

Make the ears:

Make the mask:

Make the eyes:

Make the nose:

Add details with crayons or markers.

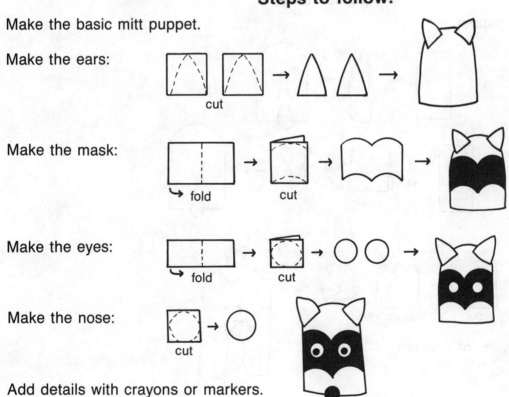

Variations:

Add a tail.

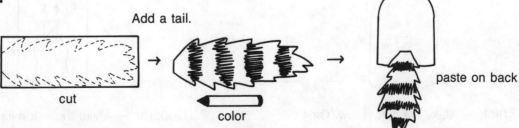

cut

color

paste on back

3   Paper Mitt Puppets

Hen

Materials:

- light brown construction paper
  basic mitt puppet—9'' x 12''
  (22.8 x 30.5cm)
- red construction paper
  wattle —2'' x 4'' (5 x 10cm)
  comb—3'' x 3'' (7.5 x 7.5cm)
- orange construction paper
  beak—2'' x 4'' (5 x 10cm)

Steps to follow:

Make the basic mitt puppet.

Make the wattle:

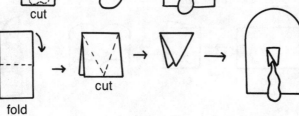

cut

Make the beak:

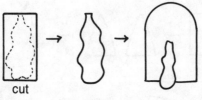

fold → cut →

Make the comb:

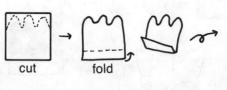

cut → fold →

Add details with crayons or markers.

Variations:

Chick — Make the mitt yellow. Omit the comb and the wattle.

Rooster — Make the mitt dark brown. Enlarge the comb and wattle.

4   Paper Mitt Puppets

Hippo

Materials:

- gray or light blue construction paper
  basic mitt puppet—9'' x 12''
    (22.8 x 30.5cm)
  ears—(Cut 2) 1½'' x 2'' (4 x 5cm)
- red construction paper
  nostrils—(Cut 2) 1½'' x 1½''
    (4 x 4cm)

Steps to follow:

Make the basic mitt puppet.

Make the ears:

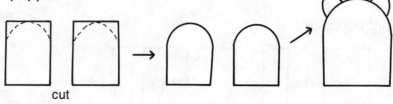

cut

Make the nostrils:

cut

Add details with crayons or markers.

Variations:

Add teeth.

Rhino — Add a horn. Omit the nostrils.

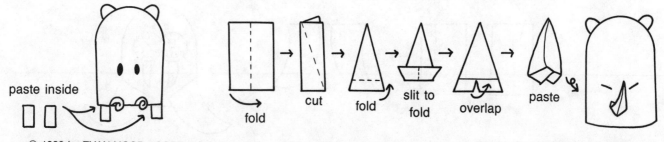

paste inside

fold

cut

fold

slit to fold

overlap

paste

5

Walrus

Materials:

- dark brown construction paper
  basic mitt puppet—9'' x 12''
  (22.8 x 30.5cm)
- light brown construction paper
  muzzle—4'' x 6'' (10 x 15cm)
- yellow construction paper
  tusks—3'' x 5'' (7.5 x 13cm)

Steps to follow:

Make the basic mitt puppet.

Make the tusks:

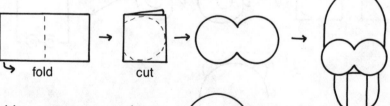

fold   cut   cut

Make the muzzle:

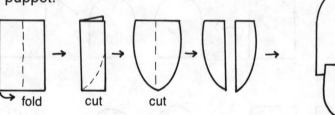

fold   cut

Add details with crayons or markers.

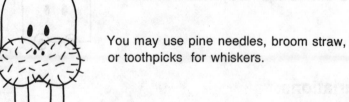

You may use pine needles, broom straw, or toothpicks for whiskers.

Variations:

Walrus with flippers — Make the tusks and the muzzle smaller. Add flippers.

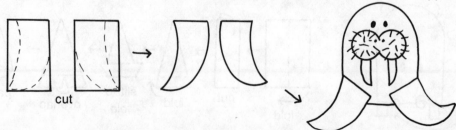

cut

6

Paper Mitt Puppets

Basic Mitt Puppet Directions

- What you need:
    — 9" x 12" (22.8 x 30.5cm) construction paper (Color varies according to puppet.)
    — Glue

- What you do:

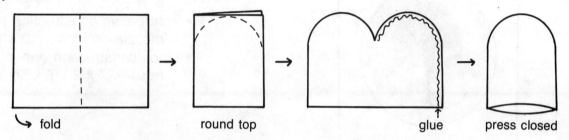

| fold | round top | glue | press closed |

Let the glue dry thoroughly while students make the other puppet parts.

- Materials needed for each puppet:
    — construction paper
    — scissors
    — glue and paste
    — crayons or felt markers

- Use your imagination. Add other extras to make the puppets sparkle:
    — buttons
    — cotton balls
    — broomstraws
    — pine needles
    — toothpicks
    — yarn
    — roving
    — raffia
    — pipe cleaners
    — feathers
    — stick-on stars or dots

© 1988 by EVAN-MOOR CORP.   1   Paper Mitt Puppets

Bear

Materials:

- dark brown construction paper
  basic mitt puppet—9'' x 12''
  (22.8 x 30.5cm)
  ears—(Cut 2) 3'' x 3'' (7.5 x 7.5cm)
- light brown construction paper
  muzzle—4'' x 4'' (10 x 10cm)
- black construction paper
  nose—2'' x 2'' (5 x 5cm)

Steps to follow:

Make the basic mitt puppet.

Make the muzzle:

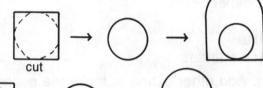

cut

Make the nose:

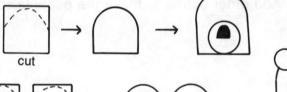

cut

Make the ears:

cut

Add details with crayons or markers.

Variations:

Mama Bear — Add a flower.

Baby Bear — Add a tongue and a bib.

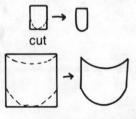

cut

Paper Mitt Puppets

Beaver

Materials:

- brown construction paper
  basic mitt puppet—9'' x 12''
    (22.8 x 30.5cm)
  ears—(Cut 2) 1½'' x 1½''
    (4 x 4cm)
  tail—4'' x 9'' (10 x 22.8cm)
- white construction paper
  teeth—1½'' x 1½'' (4 x 4cm)
- black construction paper
  nose—1½'' x 2'' (4 x 5cm)

Steps to follow:

Make the basic mitt puppet.

Make the nose:

Make the teeth:

Make the ears:

Add details with crayons or markers.

Make the tail:

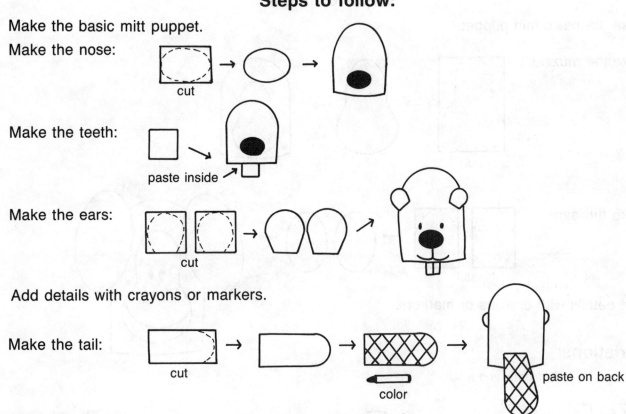

Variations:

Groundhog — Omit the tail.

back

Squirrel — Add a bushy tail.

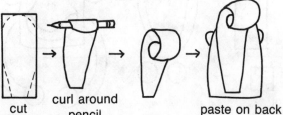

cut

curl around
pencil

paste on back

Paper Mitt Puppets

Monkey

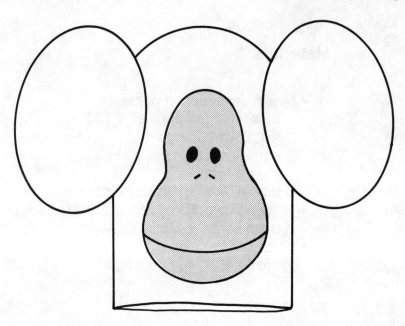

Materials:

- dark brown construction paper
  basic mitt puppet—9'' x 12''
  (22.8 x 30.5cm)
  ears—(Cut 2) 4'' x 5'' (10 x 13cm)
- Light brown construction paper
  muzzle—4½'' x 6'' (11.5 x 15cm)

Steps to follow:

Make the basic mitt puppet.

Make the muzzle:

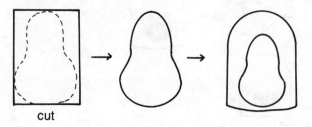

Make the ears:

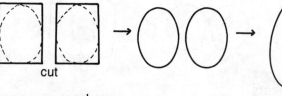

Add details with crayons or markers.

Variations:

Add arms and a tail.

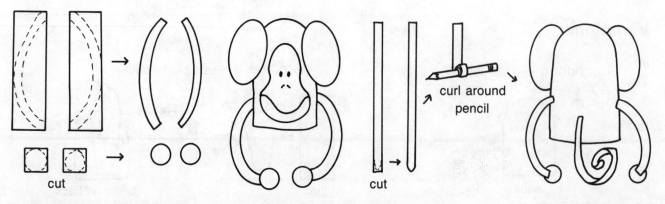

curl around
pencil

Lamb

Materials:

- white construction paper
  basic mitt puppet—9'' x 12''
  (22.8 x 30.5cm)
- black construction paper
  ears—3'' x 6'' (7.5 x 15cm) (Cut 2)
- cotton

Steps to follow:

Make the basic mitt puppet.

Make the ears:

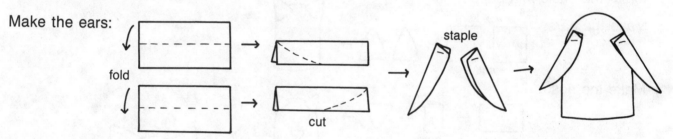

fold

cut

staple

Add details with crayons or markers.

Add cotton.

Variations:

Wooly Lamb — Cover the back with cotton.

Ram — Add horns.

cut

Paper Mitt Puppets

Cat

Materials:

- yellow construction paper
  basic mitt puppet—9'' x 12''
    (22.8 x 30.5cm)
  ears—3'' x 3'' (7.5 x 7.5cm) (Cut 2)
  tail—12'' x 1'' (30.5 x 2.5cm)
- pink construction paper
  nose—1½'' x 2'' (4 x 5cm)
- black construction paper scraps for
  whiskers

Steps to follow:

Make the basic mitt puppet.

Make the ears:

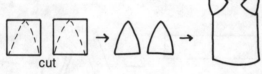

Make the nose:

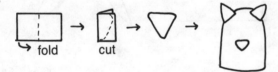

Add details with crayons or markers. Add the whiskers.

Make the tail:

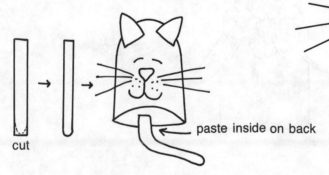

paste inside on back

Variations:

Rabbit — Make bigger ears. Add teeth and a cotton ball tail.

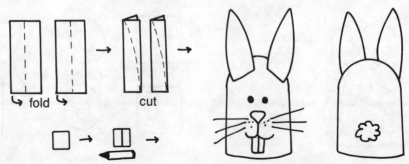

   Paper Mitt Puppets

Dog

Materials:

- white construction paper
  basic mitt puppet—9'' x 12''
  (22.8 x 30.5cm)
- black construction paper
  ears—2'' x 6'' (5 x 15cm)(Cut 2)
  eyes—1½'' x 3'' (4 x 7.5cm)
  nose—2'' x 2'' (5 x 5cm)
- pink construction paper
  tongue—1½'' x 2'' (4 x 5cm)

Steps to follow:

Make the basic mitt puppet.

Make the nose:

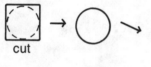

Make the eyes:

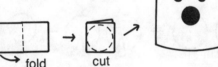

Make the ears:

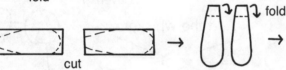

Add details with crayons or markers.

Make the tongue:

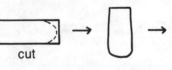

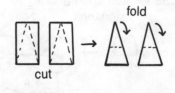

Variations:

Shaggy Dog — Add shaggy ears, a shaggy muzzle and a shaggy topknot.

Spotted Dog — Change the ears. Add a collar and spots.

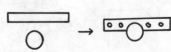

Paper Mitt Puppets

Mouse

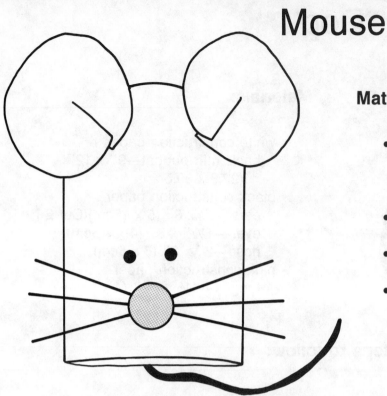

Materials:

- white or gray construction paper
  basic mitt puppet—9'' x 12''
    (22.8 x 30.5cm)
  ears—4'' x 4'' (10 x 10cm)(Cut 2)
- pink construction paper
  nose—1½'' x 1½'' (4 x 4cm)
- black construction paper scraps for whiskers
- 9'' (22.8cm) piece of yarn or roving for the tail

Steps to follow:

Make the basic mitt puppet.

Make the ears:

 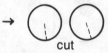 

Make the nose:

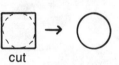

Add the whiskers.

paste on back

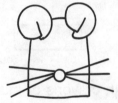

Add details with crayons or markers.

Glue the tail on the back.

Variations:

Country Mouse — Add a hat and a bandanna.

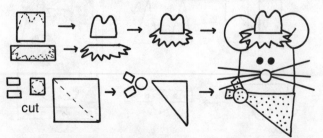

City Mouse — Add a hat, a collar, and a bow tie.

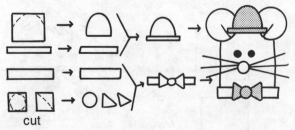

Paper Mitt Puppets

Pig

Materials:

- pink construction paper
  - basic mitt puppet—9'' x 12''
    (22.8 x 30.5cm)
  - snout—3'' x 4'' (7.5 x 10cm)
  - spacer—3'' x 1'' (7.5 x 10cm)
  - ears—(Cut 2) 2½'' x 5''
    (6.5 x 13cm)
- pipe cleaner for the tail

Steps to follow:

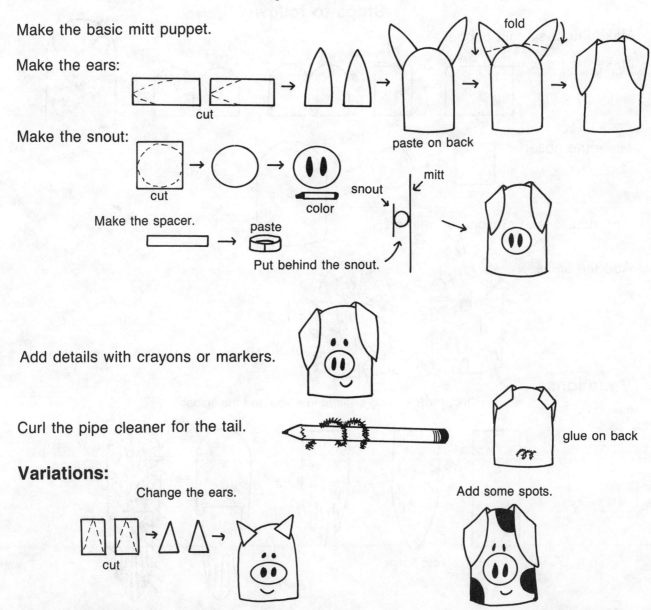

Make the basic mitt puppet.

Make the ears:

cut

Make the snout:

cut

color

Make the spacer.

paste

Put behind the snout.

snout   mitt

fold

paste on back

Add details with crayons or markers.

Curl the pipe cleaner for the tail.

glue on back

Variations:

Change the ears.

cut

Add some spots.

Hedgehog

Materials:

- brown construction paper
  basic mitt puppet—9'' x 12''
  (22.8 x 30.5cm)
  ears—1½'' x 3'' (4 x 7.5cm)
- black construction paper
  nose—1½'' x 1½'' (4 x 4cm)
- broom straws, toothpicks, or
  pine needles for spines

Steps to follow:

Make the basic mitt puppet.

Make the ears:

Make the nose:

Add details with crayons or markers.

Add the spines:

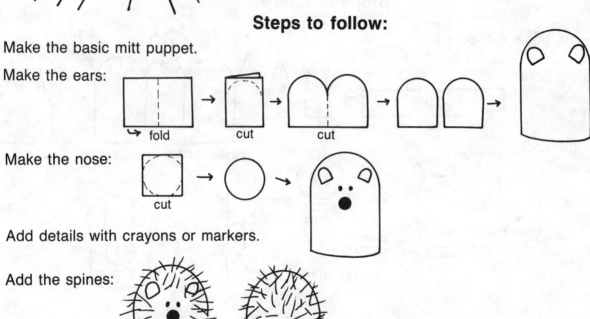

Variations:

Porcupine — Add a tail before you add the spines.

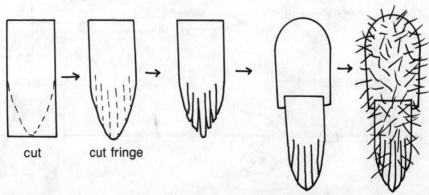

cut   cut fringe

         Paper Mitt Puppets

Turtle

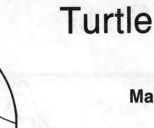

Materials:

- green construction paper
  basic mitt puppet—9'' x 12''
  (22.8 x 30.5cm)
- light green construction paper
  head—3'' x 3'' (7.5 x 7.5cm)
  neck—2'' x 4'' (5 x 10cm)
  tail—small scrap
  feet—(Cut 4) 1½'' x 2'' (4 x 5cm)

Steps to follow:

Make the basic mitt puppet.

Add details with crayons or markers.

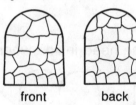

front   back

Make the head and neck:

cut   paste onto neck

Paste the bottom of the neck to the shell so the head sticks out.

Add details with crayons or markers.

Make the tail:

cut

Add the feet and the tail.

paste inside

Variations:

Sea Turtle — Change the feet to flippers.

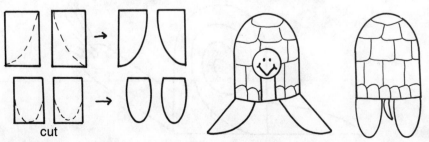

cut

Snail

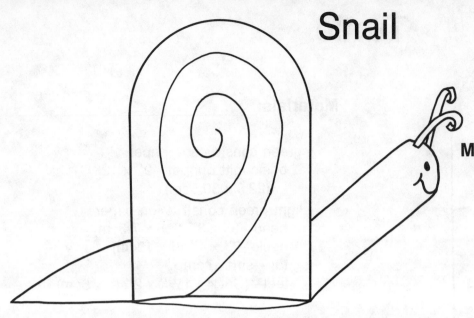

Materials:

- light green construction paper
  basic mitt puppet—9'' x 12''
  (22.8 x 30.5cm)
- yellow construction paper
  tail—2'' x 5'' (5 x 13cm)
  head—2'' x 6'' (5 x 15cm)
  feelers—scraps

Steps to follow:

Make the head:

cut

Cut the basic mitt puppet. Glue the head inside when you glue the mitt.

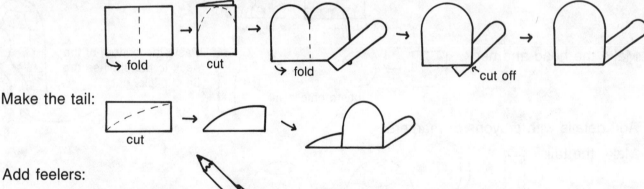

fold   cut   fold   cut off

Make the tail:

cut

Add feelers:

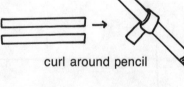

curl around pencil

Add details with crayons or markers.

Variations:

Realistic Snail —Add two short feelers and two long feelers. Color eyes on the ends of the long feelers.

Paper Mitt Puppets

Goat

Materials:

- white construction paper
  basic mitt puppet—9'' x 12''
    (22.8 x 30.5cm)
  ears—2½'' x 5'' (6.5 x 13cm)(Cut 2)
  beard—2'' x 4'' (5 x 10cm)
- yellow construction paper
  horns—2'' x 2'' (5 x 5cm)

Steps to follow:

Make the basic mitt puppet.

Make the ears:

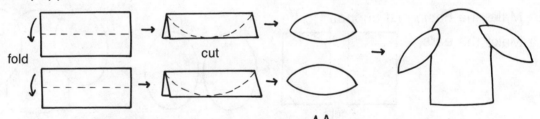

fold   cut

Make the horns:

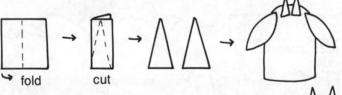

fold   cut

Make the beard:

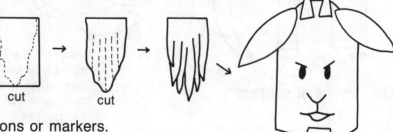

cut   cut

Add details with crayons or markers.

Variations:

Little Billy Goat —

Make the horns and the beard smaller. Change the eyes and the mouth.

Biggest Billy Goat —

Make the horns and the beard larger. Change the eyes and the mouth.

Paper Mitt Puppets

Elephant

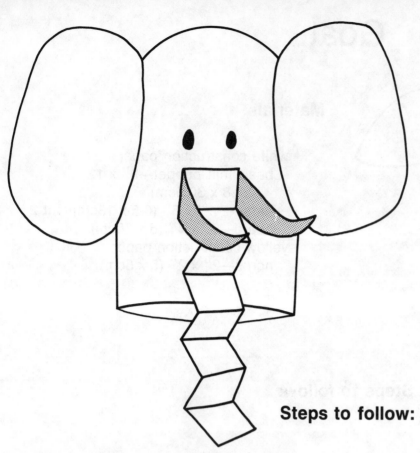

Materials:

- gray construction paper
  basic mitt puppet—9" x 12"
  (22.8 x 30.5cm)
  ears—(Cut 2) 4" x 6"
  (10 x 15cm)
  trunk—2" x 12" (5 x 30.5cm)
- white construction paper
  tusks—3" x 4" (7.5 x 10cm)

Steps to follow:

Make the basic mitt puppet.

Make the ears:

Make the trunk:

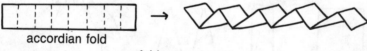
accordian fold

Make the tusks:

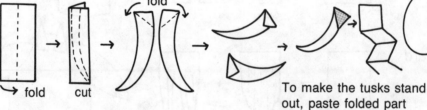

To make the tusks stand out, paste folded part behind the trunk when you paste the trunk on the puppet.

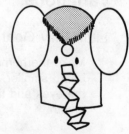

Add details with crayons or markers.

Variations:

Paste a peanut shell or some straw on the trunk. Add yarn or roving on the back for a tail.

Circus Elephant — Omit the tusks. Add a headpiece.

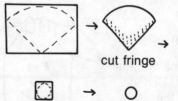
cut fringe

cut

Paper Mitt Puppets

Lion

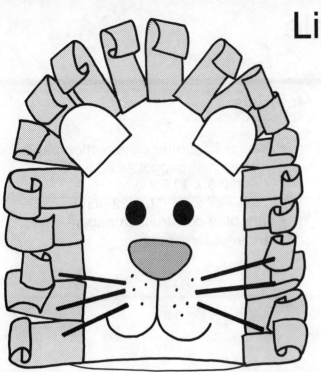

Materials:

- yellow construction paper
  basic mitt puppet—9'' x 12''
  (22.8 x 30.5cm)
  ears—(Cut 2) 2'' x 2'' (5 x 5cm)
- orange construction paper
  mane—(Cut 20 per child) 4'' x 1''
  (10 x 2.5cm)
- brown construction paper
  nose—1½'' x 2'' (4 x 5cm)
- black construction paper scraps for
  whiskers

Steps to follow:

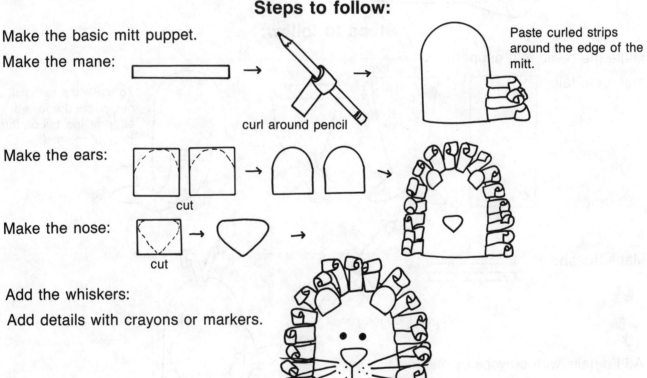

Make the basic mitt puppet.

Make the mane:

curl around pencil

Paste curled strips around the edge of the mitt.

Make the ears:

cut

Make the nose:

cut

Add the whiskers:

Add details with crayons or markers.

Variations:

Glue on yarn or roving loops for the mane.

Female Lion —
Omit the mane.

19

Paper Mitt Puppets

Whale

Materials:

- gray or light blue construction paper
  basic mitt puppet — 9'' x 12''
  (22.8 x 30.5cm)
  tail—4'' x 9'' (10 x 22.8cm)
- dark blue construction paper—thin
  strips for the spout.

Steps to follow:

Make the basic mitt puppet.

Make the tail:

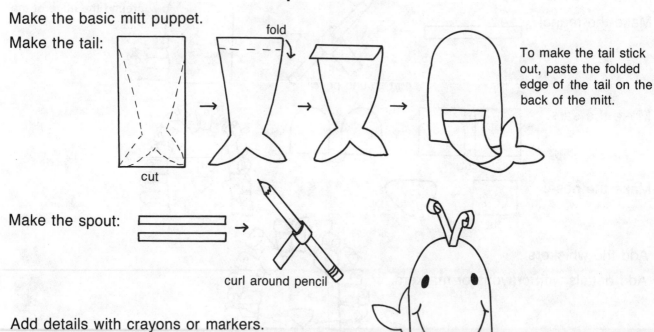

To make the tail stick out, paste the folded edge of the tail on the back of the mitt.

Make the spout:

curl around pencil

Add details with crayons or markers.

Variations:

Make a pipe cleaner spout.

Orca — Add black markings and fins. Omit the spout.

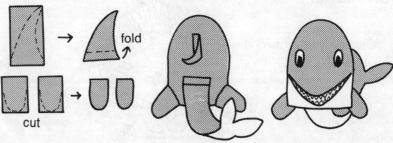

Octopus

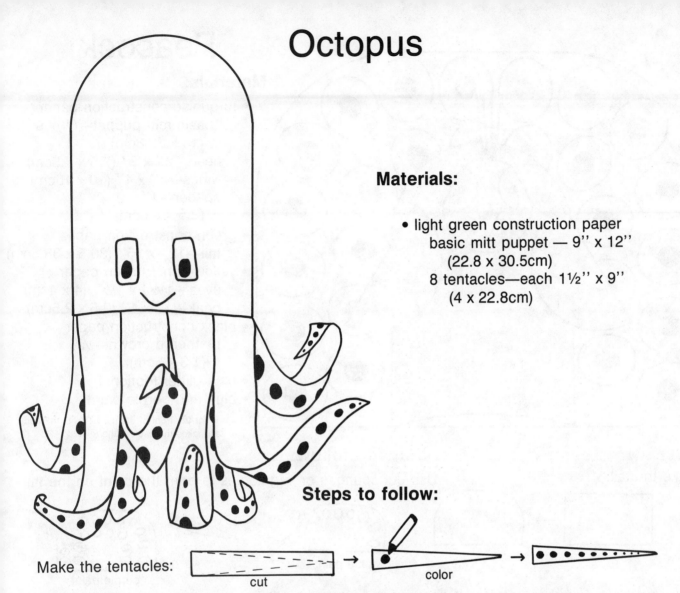

Materials:

- light green construction paper
  basic mitt puppet — 9'' x 12''
  (22.8 x 30.5cm)
  8 tentacles—each 1½'' x 9''
  (4 x 22.8cm)

Steps to follow:

Make the tentacles:

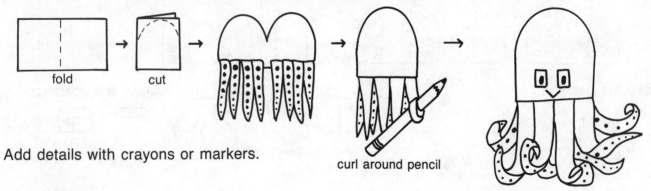

cut → color

Make the basic mitt puppet. Paste the tentacles inside before you glue the mitt.

fold → cut → → curl around pencil →

Add details with crayons or markers.

Variations:

Jellyfish —

Use waxed paper to make the mitt and the tentacles. Make the tentacles thinner and vary their lengths.

Spider — Accordian fold the legs. Add string. Change the expression.

Paper Mitt Puppets

Peacock

Materials:

- turquoise construction paper
  *basic mitt puppet—6'' x 9''
  (15 x 22.8cm)
  head—3'' x 3'' (7.5 x 7.5cm)
  wings—4'' x 4'' (10 x 10cm)
  spacer—1'' x 2½''
  (2.5 x 6.5cm)
- green construction paper
  tail—12'' x 15'' (30.5 x 38.5cm)
- yellow construction paper
  eyes—1½'' x 1½'' (4 x 4cm)
  beak—1'' x 1'' (2.5 x 2.5cm)
- black construction paper
  feathered crown—½'' x 2''
  (1.3 x 5cm)
- blue glitter (optional)
- blue and purple paint

*Cut one for the front of the mitt. This is the body.
The tail makes the back of the mitt.

Steps to follow:

Make the tail: Use cut sponges or vegetables to print the paint on the tail.

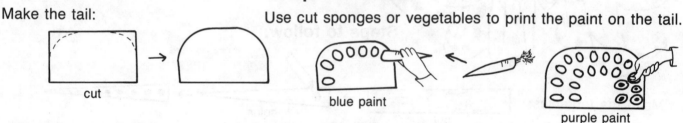

blue paint   purple paint

Make the basic mitt puppet using the body for the front and the tail as the back.

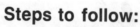

Make the head: Make the eyes: Make the spacer:

cut   cut   fold cut   head   spacer   body

Make the beak:
cut

Make the feathered crown:

cut fringe   →   add glitter

paste on back
of head

Make the wings:

cut   fold   cut

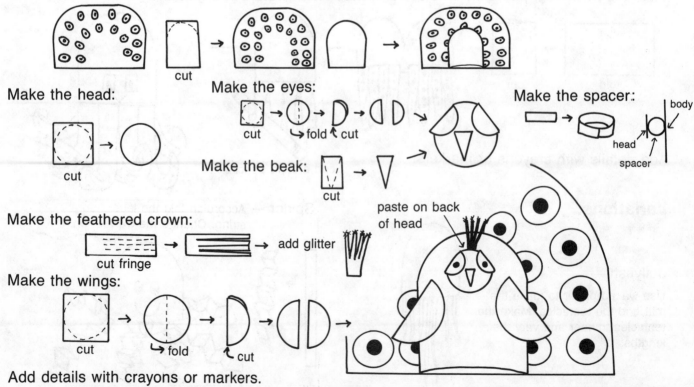

Add details with crayons or markers.

© 1988 by EVAN-MOOR CORP.   22   Paper Mitt Puppets

Car

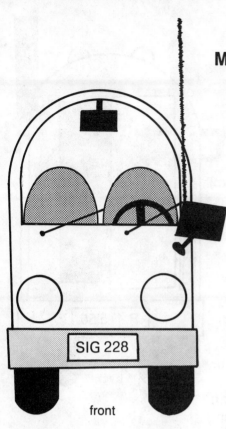

front

Materials:

- construction paper (any color)
  basic mitt puppet—9'' x 12''
  (22.8 x 30.5cm)
- white construction paper
  windshield—4'' x 5'' (10 x 13cm)
  bumpers—(Cut 2) 1'' x 6''
  (2.5 x 15cm)
  license plates—(Cut 2) 1'' x 2''
  (2.5 x 5cm)
  rear window—3'' x 4½''
  (7.5 x 11.5cm)
  rear lights—1½'' x 2'' (4 x 5cm)
- yellow construction paper
  headlights—1½'' x 3'' (4 x 7.5cm)
- black construction paper
  side mirror—1'' x 1½'' (2.5 x 4cm)
  wheels—(Cut 2) 3'' x 2'' (7.5 x 5cm)
- 6'' (15cm) strip of pipe cleaner for
  the antenna
- Aluminum foil

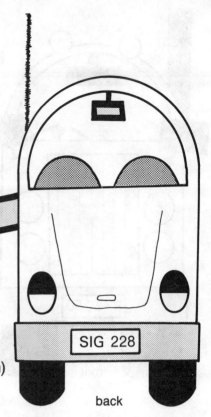

back

Steps to follow:

Make the basic mitt puppet.

Make the wheels:

Cover the bumpers with aluminum foil.

Make the windshield and rear window:

Make the side mirror:

Make the headlights:

Add the antenna.

Make the tail lights:

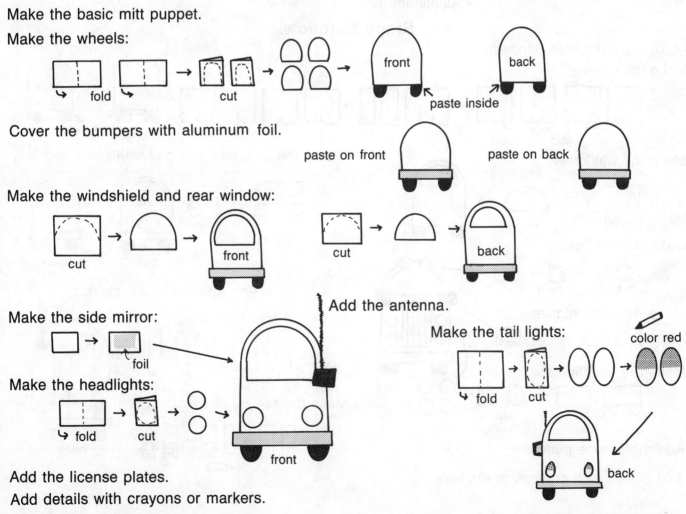

Add the license plates.

Add details with crayons or markers.

Paper Mitt Puppets

Truck

front

Materials:

- construction paper (any color)
    basic mitt puppet—9'' x 12''
        (22.8 x 30.5cm)
    rear doors—4'' x 6'' (10 x 15cm)
- white construction paper
    windshield—3'' x 5½'' (7.5 x 14cm)
    bumper—(Cut 2) 1'' x 6''
        (2.5 x 15cm)
    grill—3'' x 4'' (7.5 x 10cm)
    tail lights—1'' x 2'' (2.5 x 5cm)
    license plate—(Cut 2) 1'' x 2''
        (2.5 x 5cm)
- yellow construction paper
    headlights—(Cut 2) 1'' x 2''
        (2.5 x 5cm)
    top lights—½'' x 1½'' (1.3 x 4cm)
- black construction paper
    wheels—(Cut 4) 2'' x 2'' (5 x 5cm)
    smokestack—½'' x 4'' (1.5 x 10cm)
    side mirrors—(Cut 2) 1½'' x 1''
        (4 x 2.5cm)
- Aluminum foil

Steps to follow:

Make the basic mitt puppet.

Make the wheels:

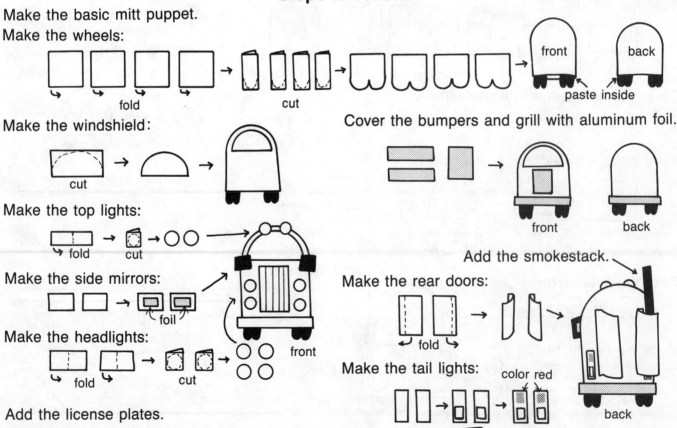

Make the windshield:

Make the top lights:

Make the side mirrors:

Make the headlights:

Add the license plates.

Add details with crayons or markers.

Cover the bumpers and grill with aluminum foil.

Add the smokestack.

Make the rear doors:

Make the tail lights:

24   Paper Mitt Puppets

Spaceship

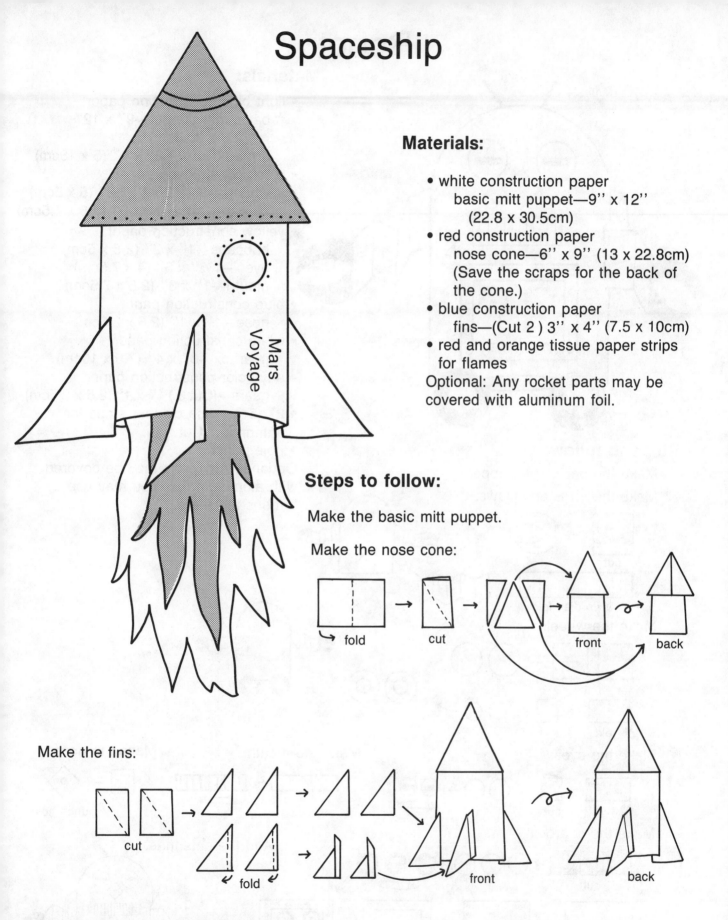

Materials:

- white construction paper
  basic mitt puppet—9'' x 12''
  (22.8 x 30.5cm)
- red construction paper
  nose cone—6'' x 9'' (13 x 22.8cm)
  (Save the scraps for the back of
  the cone.)
- blue construction paper
  fins—(Cut 2) 3'' x 4'' (7.5 x 10cm)
- red and orange tissue paper strips
  for flames

Optional: Any rocket parts may be
covered with aluminum foil.

Steps to follow:

Make the basic mitt puppet.

Make the nose cone:

fold → cut → front → back

Make the fins:

cut → fold → front → back

Add details with crayons or markers.

Add the flames.

Mars Voyage

Robot

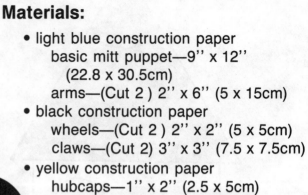

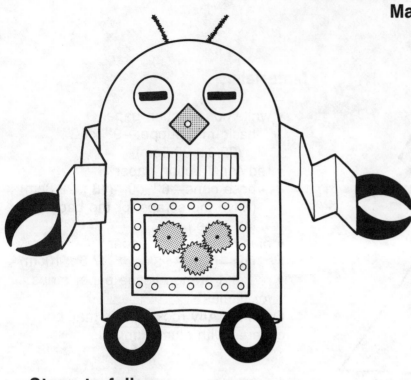

Materials:

- light blue construction paper
  - basic mitt puppet—9'' x 12'' (22.8 x 30.5cm)
  - arms—(Cut 2) 2'' x 6'' (5 x 15cm)
- black construction paper
  - wheels—(Cut 2) 2'' x 2'' (5 x 5cm)
  - claws—(Cut 2) 3'' x 3'' (7.5 x 7.5cm)
- yellow construction paper
  - hubcaps—1'' x 2'' (2.5 x 5cm)
  - eyes—1½'' x 3'' (4 x 7.5cm)
  - mouth—1'' x 3'' (2.5 x 7.5cm)
- blue construction paper
  - nose—1'' x 1'' (2.5 x 2.5cm)
- white construction paper
  - gearbox—3'' x 4'' (7.5 x 10cm)
- any color construction paper
  - gears—(Cut 3) 1'' x 1'' (2.5 x 2.5cm)
- 2'' (5cm) pipe cleaner strips for antennae. (Cut 2)
- hole punch

Optional: Any parts may be covered with aluminum foil. You may use buttons for gears.

Steps to follow:

Make the basic mitt puppet.

Make the arms and claws:

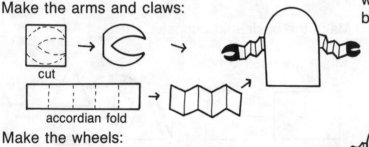

Make the wheels:

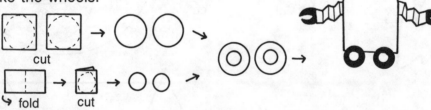

Make the eyes:

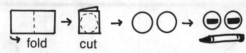

Make the mouth:

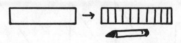

Make the nose:

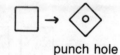
punch hole

Make the gearbox:

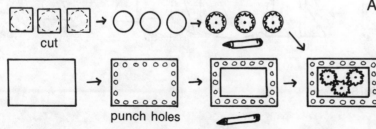
punch holes

Add the antennae.

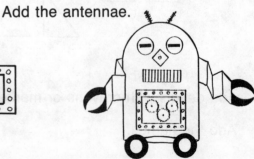

Add details with crayons or markers.

Paper Mitt Puppets

Astronaut

Earth

Materials:

- construction paper (any color)
  basic mitt puppet—9'' x 12''
  (22.8 x 30.5cm)
  air hose—1½'' x 12'' (4 x 30.5cm)
- white construction paper
  face—3'' x 4'' (7.5 x 10cm)
  speaker, ear piece, air hose
  holder—(Cut 3) 1'' x 2'' (2.5 x 5cm)
- 5'' x 5'' (13 x 13cm) clear plastic for
  face mask. Cut it from heavy plastic
  storage bags.
- ½'' masking tape or colored tape
- Aluminum foil

Steps to follow:

Make the basic mitt puppet.

Add the face:

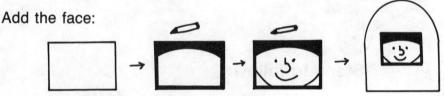

Add details with crayons or markers.

Tape on the plastic face mask.

Cover the speaker, the ear piece, and the air hose holder with aluminum foil.

Glue foil-covered pieces on helmet.

Make the air hose:

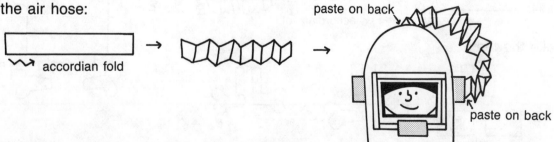

accordian fold

paste on back

paste on back

Paper Mitt Puppets

Space Creature

Materials:

- green construction paper
  basic mitt puppet—9'' x 12''
    (22.8 x 30.5cm)
  arms—(Cut 4) 1'' x 6'' (2.5 x 15cm)
- yellow construction paper
  mouth—3'' x 4'' (7.5 x 10cm)
  eyes—(Cut 2) 2'' x 2'' (5 x 5cm)
  eye holders—(Cut 2) ½'' x 2½''
    (1.3 x 6.5cm)
- purple construction paper
  legs—(Cut 2) 1'' x 3'' (2.5 x 7.5cm)
  feet—(Cut 2) 3'' x 4'' (7.5 x 10cm)
  polka dots—available scraps
- 2'' (5cm) strip of pipe cleaner for the
  antenna.

Steps to follow:

Make the basic mitt puppet.

Make the eyes:

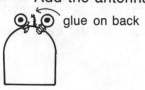

Add the antenna.

glue on back

accordian fold

Make the mouth:

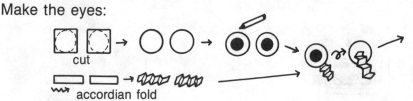

cut

Add details with crayons or markers.

Make the arms.

cut   accordian fold

Make the feet:

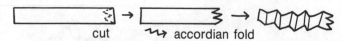

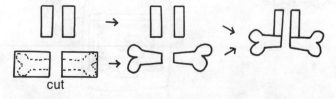

cut

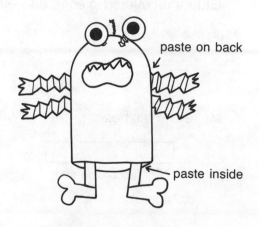

paste on back

paste inside

Add the polka dots.

Paper Mitt Puppets

Dragon

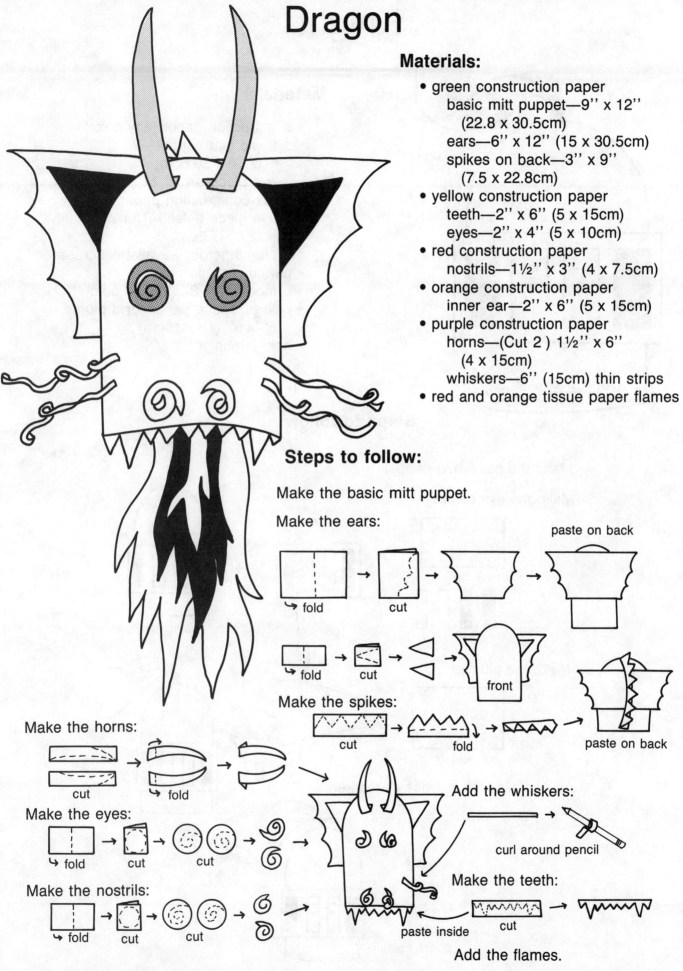

Materials:

- green construction paper
  basic mitt puppet—9'' x 12''
     (22.8 x 30.5cm)
  ears—6'' x 12'' (15 x 30.5cm)
  spikes on back—3'' x 9''
     (7.5 x 22.8cm)
- yellow construction paper
  teeth—2'' x 6'' (5 x 15cm)
  eyes—2'' x 4'' (5 x 10cm)
- red construction paper
  nostrils—1½'' x 3'' (4 x 7.5cm)
- orange construction paper
  inner ear—2'' x 6'' (5 x 15cm)
- purple construction paper
  horns—(Cut 2) 1½'' x 6''
     (4 x 15cm)
  whiskers—6'' (15cm) thin strips
- red and orange tissue paper flames

Steps to follow:

Make the basic mitt puppet.

Make the ears:

fold → cut → → paste on back

fold → cut → → front → paste on back

Make the spikes:

cut → fold →

Make the horns:

cut → fold →

Make the eyes:

fold → cut → cut →

Make the nostrils:

fold → cut → cut →

Add the whiskers:

curl around pencil

Make the teeth:

cut →

paste inside

Add the flames.

Knight

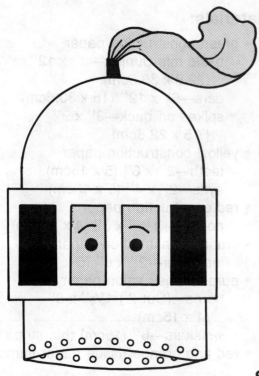

Materials:

- construction paper (any color)
  basic mitt puppet—9'' x 12''
    (22.8 x 30.5cm)
  eye piece—4'' x 7'' (10 x 7cm)
- black construction paper
  eye piece holes—(Cut 2) 1'' x 3''
    (2.5 x 7.5cm)
  plume holder—available scraps
- tan construction paper
  face—1'' x 3'' (2.5 x 7.5cm)
- colored tissue paper for a plume
  5'' x 6'' (13 x 15cm)
- hole punch

Steps to follow:

Make the basic mitt puppet.

Make the eye piece:

Make the plume:

Add details with crayons or markers.

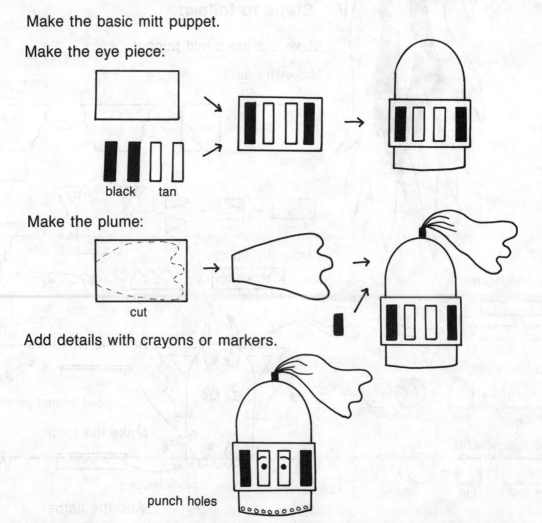

black   tan

cut

punch holes

Princess

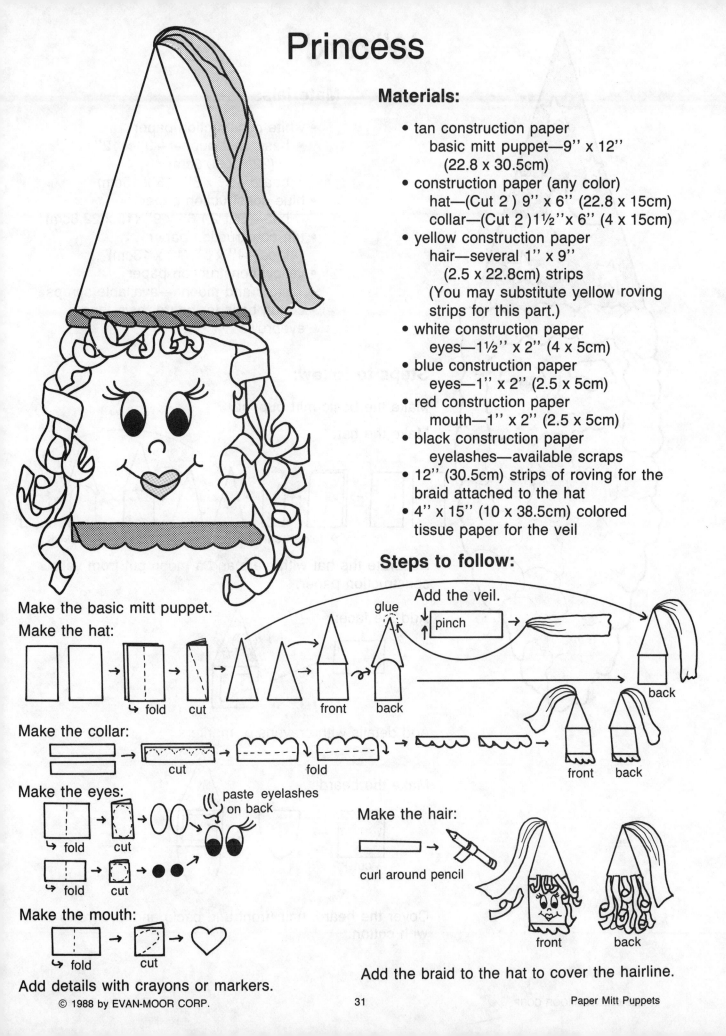

Materials:

- tan construction paper
  basic mitt puppet—9'' x 12''
  (22.8 x 30.5cm)
- construction paper (any color)
  hat—(Cut 2) 9'' x 6'' (22.8 x 15cm)
  collar—(Cut 2)1½''x 6'' (4 x 15cm)
- yellow construction paper
  hair—several 1'' x 9''
  (2.5 x 22.8cm) strips
  (You may substitute yellow roving
  strips for this part.)
- white construction paper
  eyes—1½'' x 2'' (4 x 5cm)
- blue construction paper
  eyes—1'' x 2'' (2.5 x 5cm)
- red construction paper
  mouth—1'' x 2'' (2.5 x 5cm)
- black construction paper
  eyelashes—available scraps
- 12'' (30.5cm) strips of roving for the
  braid attached to the hat
- 4'' x 15'' (10 x 38.5cm) colored
  tissue paper for the veil

Steps to follow:

Make the basic mitt puppet.

Make the hat:

fold   cut   front   back

Add the veil.
glue
pinch
back
front   back

Make the collar:

cut   fold   front   back

Make the eyes:

fold   cut   paste eyelashes on back

fold   cut

Make the mouth:

fold   cut

Add details with crayons or markers.

Make the hair:

curl around pencil   front   back

Add the braid to the hat to cover the hairline.

© 1988 by EVAN-MOOR CORP.

31

Paper Mitt Puppets

Wizard

Materials:

- white construction paper
  basic mitt puppet—9'' x 12''
     (22.8 x 30.5cm)
  beard—6'' x 6'' (15 x 15cm)
- blue construction paper
  hat—(Cut 2) 6'' x 9'' (15 x 22.8cm)
- tan construction paper
  face—4'' x 5'' (10 x 13cm)
- yellow construction paper
  stars and moons—available scraps
- cotton balls for beard, hair, and
  eyebrows

Steps to follow:

Make the basic mitt puppet.

Make the hat:

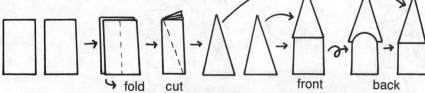

Decorate the hat with stars and a moon cut from yellow construction paper.

Add the face:

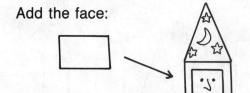

Add details with crayons or markers.

Make the beard:

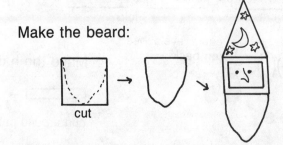

Cover the beard, hair (front and back), and eyebrows with cotton.

Paper Mitt Puppets